DECODING THE PSYCHOLOGY OF MONEY

Empower Your Wealth: Navigate Financial Terrain with Insight"

DR. JAKE JAYLEN

INTRODUCTION

Greetings from a journey beyond conventional money management guides: one of self-discovery and financial empowerment. We'll untangle the complex dance between the mind and money in the following pages, giving you the tools you need to negotiate the financial landscape with a fresh perspective. This is your guide to understanding the psychology of money and changing how you interact with your wealth; it's not simply another book about finance.

The Need: Unlocking Financial Wisdom

Many of us long for a more profound comprehension of our connection with money in a world where financial decisions frequently feel like a puzzle lacking a few pieces. You may be an experienced investor hoping to escape the emotional rollercoaster of the markets, or you may be a young professional ready to lay the groundwork for your financial future. This book is designed to meet you where you are, no matter who you are or where you are in life.

The Pain Point: Breaking Free from the Money Maze

Have you ever had doubts about your financial decisions and wondered why you choose to take particular actions with your money? It's not just you. The conflict is real, and it frequently has its roots in unconscious psychological forces that affect how we view, approach, and manage our money. Your guide to solving these puzzles and resolving any pain spots that might be preventing you from achieving true financial success is "Decoding the Psychology of Money."

The Desire: Empower Your Wealth

Imagine leading a life in which you are confidently able to make financial decisions because you are well-informed about the invisible forces at play. One day, imagine, that money will be working for you instead of against you. This is not just a pipe dream;

it may actually be your reality. Rather than just helping you get rich, the goal of this book is to empower your money by showing you how to become a skilled financial decision-maker.

The Aspiration: Mastering the Mind-Money Connection

Our goal is straightforward yet profound: we want you to understand the relationship between mind and money. As you set out on this trip, you'll learn about your personal financial attitude, how to handle the delicate emotional aspects of investing, and practical techniques for making wise financial choices. This book serves as a companion in your quest for long-term prosperity, your passport to financial resilience, and your road map to realizing your goals.

'Decoding the Psychology of Money' is therefore designed to meet you where you are and guide you toward where you want to be, whether you're a fresh graduate entering the job, a family navigating the complexities of shared finances, or an experienced investor trying to strengthen your methods. Are you prepared to open the locks on your wallet and set off on a life-changing path toward financial independence? Together, let's turn the page and embark on the adventure. These chapters hold the power to mold your money, which is waiting for you.

CHAPTER ONE

The Psychology-Money Connection

Welcome to an exploration of the deep connection between the human mind and the financial world that goes beyond traditional financial knowledge and goes beyond figures and charts. We set out to unravel the complex dance between psychology and financial decision-making in this first chapter—a relationship that is sometimes missed in the din of financial advice.

Setting the Stage

Numbers frequently take center stage in the vast field of personal finance. Of course, budgets, investments, and returns are all important factors. However, there is a psychological dimension to our financial decisions and the unseen force that shapes our economic fates. Knowing this connection is a transformative path toward financial empowerment, not just an intellectual one.

Mission: Empowerment through Insight

"Decoding the Psychology of Money" is more than simply a book; it's a declaration of intent, an appeal to action for people who want to better understand themselves in relation to money as well as achieve financial success. Our goal is to provide you with knowledge that goes beyond the cliches associated with investing and budgeting. Our goal is to provide you the knowledge and skills necessary to confidently and intelligently negotiate the treacherous world of financial decision-making.

The Mindset Effect on Financial Achievement

Ever wonder why two people with comparable financial resources may have such dissimilar experiences? Their mentality frequently holds the solution. Your attitudes, ideas, and perceptions of money serve as the basis for your financial choices.

We will explore the subtle but potent ways that your thinking may either help you achieve financial success or become a roadblock as we dive into the psychology of money.

Navigating the Uncharted Waters

One does not make financial decisions in a vacuum. Numerous factors—some obvious, others deeply embedded in our psyche—have an impact on them. We'll go into the idea of behavioral finance, a discipline that acknowledges the role that people have in financial decisions. Gaining insight into the behavioral biases and heuristics that affect decision-making gives you a better sense of direction as you negotiate the frequently choppy waters of the financial markets.

A Glimpse into Key Psychological Concepts

We'll explore how your background, society, and social standards influence your financial beliefs as we crack open the mysteries of money mindsets. We'll take you on an emotional journey through the world of investing, exploring how fear, greed, and overconfidence can affect your financial choices. But the goal of this book is to offer workable solutions, not only to identify issues. You will learn tactical methods for making wise decisions regardless of any mental obstacles you may encounter.

Your Personal Invitation

This book isn't about giving you all the answers; instead, it's about giving you the right questions and the resources to answer them for yourself. Whether you're a recent graduate entering the workforce, an aspiring investor looking for clarity, or a seasoned professional aiming for financial mastery, consider this your personal invitation to a transformative experience.

Let the pages that follow serve as your tour guide into the unexplored area where psychology and money converge, as I wrap up this introductory chapter. The trip could make you reevaluate your assumptions, spark self-discovery moments, and finally bring you to a level of financial knowledge that goes beyond popular wisdom. Settle in; the journey is about to begin. This is "Decoding the Psychology of Money." Welcome.

CHAPTER TWO

Behavioral Finance

Greetings from the intriguing field of behavioral finance. This chapter explores the psychological aspects of human financial decision-making. Gaining an insight into these subtleties can help you better navigate the complicated world of money management.

The Foundation of Behavioral Finance

First, let's lay the groundwork for behavioral finance. Examine the history of this field, following its development from psychology and conventional finance. Recognize why combining these disciplines is necessary to understand financial behavior holistically.

The Human Element in Financial Decision-Making

Examine the human factor, which lies at the core of behavioral finance. Find out how our financial decisions are influenced by our emotions and cognitive processes. Understand how biases and heuristics in the banking industry can result in both predictable and unpredictable consequences.

Biases That Impact Financial Decisions

Examine the most prevalent biases that affect financial judgment. Examine how these biases affect our perceptions of risk and reward, from overconfidence to loss aversion. Examples from real life demonstrate how these biases affect investing methods.

The Role of Heuristics in Finance

Heuristics, often known as mental shortcuts, are essential for making decisions. Analyze how heuristics can make difficult financial decisions easier to make, yet they can also make mistakes. Learn how to identify and handle these quick cuts to improve your financial literacy.

The Influence of Framing

Learn how framing—the presentation of information—can have a big influence on how decisions are made. Examine papers and experiments that demonstrate how framing might influence financial decisions. Discover how to identify and deal with the framing effect in different financial situations.

Behavioral Economics in Action

Behavioral economics serves as a link between psychology and conventional economics. Explore how policymakers might use behavioral economics' practical applications to create financial interventions that are more successful. Recognize the effects on how you personally make financial decisions.

The Psychology of Market Bubbles and Crashes

Analyze the psychological causes of market collapses and bubbles. Examine past instances to comprehend the ways in which collective actions lead to these occurrences. Learn how being aware of these trends can help you make more informed investing decisions amid erratic market situations.

Prospect Theory and its Implications

Prospect Theory transformed our comprehension of making decisions in the face of uncertainty. Examine the main ideas and ramifications of this innovative theory. Discover how prospect theory affects financial decisions and how to manage its consequences by learning how it explains deviations from rational decision-making.

Overcoming Behavioral Biases

A study of behavioral finance cannot be considered thorough if it does not examine methods for overcoming prejudice. This section offers helpful hints and methods for reducing the negative effects of emotional and cognitive biases. Give yourself the tools you need to make wiser financial decisions.

Key Takeaways

Let's review the main ideas covered in this chapter, consider the value of comprehending the behavioral finance landscape and how it may help you manage your money more strategically and perceptively, and get ready to put these teachings into practice in the upcoming chapters.

CHAPTER THREE

Money Mindsets

Welcome to your journey through "Money Mindsets." This chapter explores your ingrained attitudes and beliefs regarding money and how they influence the way you make financial decisions. One of the most important first steps to financial empowerment is realizing your money perspective.

Money Mindsets

Your perspective and interactions with money are shaped by your money attitude. We dissect the idea, talking about how your experiences, cultural influences, and upbringing shaped your particular set of financial ideas.

The Impact of Upbringing on Money Mindsets

Your financial outlook is greatly influenced by your family. Examine the impact of early life experiences, parental financial attitudes, and family financial practices. Find out how these early teachings still influence your current financial decisions in subtle ways.

Cultural and Societal Influences

Your financial perspective is greatly influenced by societal and cultural influences in addition to familial dynamics. We look at how your financial attitudes are shaped by media images of wealth, cultural standards, and society expectations.

Identifying Your Money Mindset

Set off on a quest for introspection. Discover your personal money perspective with these introspective activities and thought-provoking questions. Making aware financial decisions starts with acknowledging your ingrained money-related attitudes.

Common Money Mindsets

Explore common archetypes of money mindsets, such as the saver, spender, avoider, or risk-taker. Understand the strengths and potential pitfalls associated with each mindset and how they influence your financial choices.

Shifting Your Money Mindset

Learn about the transformative power. This section offers doable tactics to help you change your financial mindset to one that is stronger and more positive. Discover how to break through restricting ideas and develop a mindset that supports your financial objectives.

The Dynamic Money Mindset

Money mindsets change with time; they are not static. Recognize how significant life events, job shifts, and financial successes and disappointments can affect your attitude about money. Gain the ability to grow and adjust as a result of these developments, developing a strong and optimistic financial outlook.

CHAPTER FOUR

The Emotional Rollercoaster of Investing

Riding the Waves: Emotions in Investment

Even if investing is guided by statistics, graphs, and financial projections, human emotions have a significant impact. The financial markets are a theater of emotions where fear, greed, and ecstasy take center stage, not just a battlefield for economic forces. This chapter will take us on a tour through the complex web of emotions that make up an investor's experience, showing us how these feelings affect choices and, in the end, the performance of investments.

The Emotional Triggers in Investing

Fear and Panic

Fear is one of the strongest feelings when it comes to investing. Fear has the ability to immobilize even the most seasoned investors, whether it comes from a precipitous decline in the market or a financial catastrophe. Fear of losing money frequently causes people to make rash actions, such as selling off investments at the wrong moment or giving up well-considered plans in a last-ditch effort to save what's left.

Fear and Panic: The Dominance of Loss Aversion

Fear and panic are frequently the result of loss aversion, a cognitive bias in which people experience the anguish of losses more keenly than the joy of victories. Fear of losing money when investing can set off panic attacks, causing investors to act rashly and irrationally.

Impact on Decision-Making:

Herd Mentality: In the financial markets, fear has a swift way of spreading, causing investors to hurry to sell their holdings out of fear of suffering worse losses.

Impulsive Actions: Even when an investment has solid fundamentals, the fear of missing out can lead to rash decisions like selling stocks at a loss to prevent additional drops.

- **Speculative Behavior:** Speculative conduct, in which investors invest based on hype and momentum rather than fundamental examination, can be fueled by euphoria.

Managing Greed:

Diversification:

Investing across a variety of asset classes can help control risk and avoid becoming overly exposed to a single, avaricious investment.

Discipline: The temptation to chase short-term returns can be restrained by establishing defined investment goals and following a disciplined investment plan.

Regret Aversion: The Fear of Missed Opportunities

The dread of making the wrong choice and feeling guilty afterwards is known as regret aversion. Remorse averse investors may be reluctant to take important financial decisions because they are afraid of making mistakes.

Impact on Decision-Making:

Inaction: A dread of making financial decisions brought on by regret aversion might lead to missed opportunities for portfolio optimization.

Status Quo Bias: Fearing they might regret selling, investors may opt to hold onto their current investments even if the market or their financial objectives have altered.

Risk-Benefit Analysis: The influence of regret aversion can be lessened by weighing the advantages and disadvantages of choices in order to establish a more logical foundation for action.

Continuous Learning: Maintaining current market knowledge and participating in continuous financial education can boost decision-making confidence and reduce regret-related anxiety.

Harnessing Emotional Triggers for Informed Decision-Making

Although emotions are a part of investing, investors can make better judgments if they are aware of and can control their emotional triggers. Understanding the effects of greed, regret aversion, and fear lays the groundwork for creating mitigation techniques. To help investors manage the emotional rollercoaster of investing with resilience and clarity, we'll look at practical exercises and approaches to improve emotional intelligence in the field of finance in the next part.

Strategies for Managing Emotional Swings

Cultivating Emotional Intelligence

Emotional intelligence and self-control are essential for effective investing. Understanding, controlling, and being empathetic to others' feelings are all components of emotional intelligence. Investors who develop their emotional intelligence are better equipped to withstand market swings and base their choices on reasoned considerations rather than gut feelings.

Building a Resilient Mindset

Developing a resilient mindset requires first realizing that market ups and downs are inevitable. Rather than viewing downturns as failures, resilient investors view them as opportunities for growth and learning. Investors are better equipped to withstand market fluctuations and stay committed to their long-term objectives because to this shift in viewpoint.

Case Studies in Emotional Investing

The Financial Crisis of 2008: Extreme Fear Analyzing investors' emotional reactions during the 2008 financial crisis yields insightful information. When the market finally recovered, some who had remained calm profited from the sale of their portfolios during the worst of the recession. The influence of fear and the benefits of disciplined investing are demonstrated in this case study.

The Dot-Com Bubble: Lessons from Euphoria

The late 1990s Dot-Com bubble is a prime illustration of euphoria-driven investing. Investors' aggregate greed drove companies with little substance to be valued at astronomical amounts. Those who had given in to the enthusiasm lost a lot of money when the bubble burst. This case study emphasizes how crucial it is to use reason to control greed.

Strategies for Leveraging Emotional Factors

Contrarian Investing

Investors that are contrarians profit from market sentiment. They perceive opportunities for valuable investments when fear is widespread. On the other hand, contrarians exercise caution and may profit during euphoric periods. Discipline and a contrarian mentality that defies the emotions of the market are necessary for this technique.

Methodical Investing that is systematic, or rules-based, reduces emotional volatility by using pre-established methods and procedures. This strategy lessens the effects of snap judgments and encourages investors to stick with their plans even in volatile market environments.

The secret to navigating the emotional rollercoaster of investing is not to suppress feelings but to recognize them, control them, and use them to your advantage while making choices. This chapter seeks to provide readers with the knowledge and skills necessary to respond resiliently and with confidence to the highs and lows of the financial markets by examining case studies, techniques, and the psychology of emotional investment.

The impact of fear and greed on investment decisions will be discussed in more detail in the following part, along with useful exercises to improve emotional intelligence in the finance industry.

Strategies for Leveraging Emotional Factors

Contrarian Investing: Riding Against the Tide

One method that takes advantage of the market's emotional extremes is contrarian investing. Contrarian investors, as opposed to followers of the herd, buy when others are selling in panic or sell when others are buying in ecstasy. This strategy is based on the idea that markets frequently overreact to news and events, which presents chances for shrewd investors.

Key Principles:

Buy Low, Sell High: In order to sell when market sentiment turns more optimistic, contrarians look for assets that have been undervalued as a result of market pessimism.

Discipline in the Face of Fear: Acting contrary to popular opinion takes discipline, particularly when fear is rampant. The methods used by contrarians are in-depth research and a strong dedication to their investment thesis.

Example:

Investors who are contrarian may be able to spot fundamentally sound companies whose stock prices have been disproportionately impacted by a market downturn brought on by a worldwide economic crisis. They position themselves for possible long-term gains when the market rebounds by purchasing these stocks at a discount.

Systematic Investing: Rules-Based Discipline

By using preset rules and algorithms, systematic investing—often linked to quantitative or algorithmic strategies—aims to exclude emotion from investment decisions. This method is based on the idea that a methodical, disciplined approach can produce more consistent results and that human emotions might cause people to make irrational decisions.

Key Principles:

Automated Decision-Making: Systematic investors base their purchase and sell choices on pre-established criteria, and they do this by using models and algorithms. This lessens the influence of sentimental prejudices.

Consistency over Emotion: Systematic investors strive to be consistent in their approach by adhering to a set of principles and avoiding emotional responses to transient market swings.

Example: An algorithm that takes into account several financial indicators, economic data, and market patterns might be created by a systematic investor. In order to ensure that decisions are made based on data rather than gut feelings in response to market news, the algorithm automatically initiates buy or sell orders when specific circumstances are satisfied.

Dollar-Cost Averaging: Smoothing Out the Bumps

Regardless of market conditions, dollar-cost averaging is a method that includes regularly investing a set amount of money at regular intervals. This strategy works well to lessen the effects of momentary market fluctuations and subjective judgments.

Key Principles:

Consistent Contributions: Regardless of market conditions, investors make a certain number of contributions at regular periods, such as monthly or quarterly.

Purchasing More at Low Prices: During times of market declines, the fixed investment amount purchases more shares, gradually bringing down the average price per share.

Example: An investor makes a monthly commitment to invest $500 in a specific stock. The $500 purchases more shares when the price of the stock is low and fewer shares when it is high. This approach seeks to offer a more measured and dispassionate introduction to the market over time.

Embracing Emotional Factors for Informed Decision-Making

Although various tactics make different use of emotional elements, they all aim to transform emotions from possible drawbacks into tactical advantages. Through a comprehension of the affective aspects of investing and the utilization of tactics that leverage market mood, investors can man oeuvre through the turbulent terrain with an increased feeling of command and intention. The goal is to use emotions to help you make informed and logical financial decisions, not to get rid of them.

CHAPTER FIVE

Financial Decision-Making Strategies

Making wise decisions is crucial for success in both personal and professional efforts in the dynamic and complex world of today. The capacity to successfully gather, evaluate, and understand information is essential whether navigating the complexities of business decisions, determining a course for career progression, or just making judgments on a daily basis that are consistent with our beliefs and objectives.

Defining Informed Choices

A decision that is made after a thorough analysis of all pertinent information, available options, and potential outcomes is considered informed. Instead of being an arbitrary estimate or an instinctive reaction, it is a thoughtful assessment supported by solid logic and data. Making informed decisions is not always simple since it frequently calls for us to go outside of our comfort zones, question our presumptions, and take into account viewpoints that differ from our own. Making educated decisions can, however, pay off greatly since it can result in better outcomes, more self-assurance, and a feeling of empowerment.

Strategic Approaches to Informed Choices

There are a number of tactical methods that can improve our capacity for deliberation.

Gathering Information:

Getting as much pertinent information as you can is the first step towards making an informed decision. This could entail gathering information through research, talking to authorities, and getting input from others. It's critical to exercise discernment when choosing information sources, making sure they are trustworthy, objective, and current..

Analyzing Information:

After gathering data, it is imperative that we critically evaluate it in order to spot patterns, trends, and any ramifications. This could entail identifying areas of uncertainty, highlighting important findings, and arranging data into tables or figures.

Considering Options:

We must weigh all of the possibilities after evaluating the data and any possible repercussions. This could entail doing a cost-benefit analysis, coming up with a decision matrix, or brainstorming.

Evaluating Outcomes:

Once the data has been analyzed, we must weigh every choice that is accessible and any potential repercussions. This may include coming up with ideas on the spot, making a decision matrix, or running a cost-benefit analysis.

Making a Decision:

Once we have thoroughly considered our options, we must decide and stick with it. This could entail telling people about our choice and moving forward with its implementation.

Monitoring and Adapting:

We must keep an eye on our choices and be ready to modify course when needed as conditions change. This could entail getting fresh data, reevaluating our options, and modifying our original plans.

Enhancing Informed Decision-Making

In addition to these strategic approaches, there are several other things we can do to enhance our ability to make informed choices:

Cultivate a curious mindset: Strive to find information that contradicts your presumptions and keep an open mind to fresh viewpoints.

Develop critical thinking skills: Inquire about facts, recognize prejudices, and consider the evidence impartially.

- **Practice effective communication:** Possess the ability to communicate your ideas succinctly and clearly, as well as to actively hear other people out.

- **Recognize and manage biases:** Recognize your personal prejudices and how they could affect the choices you make.

- **Seek feedback:** Ask for input from others on a regular basis to discover new viewpoints and blind spots.

- **Learn from experience:** In order to pinpoint opportunities for development and formulate plans for upcoming decisions, consider past decisions.

- Making wise decisions requires lifelong learning and development. Through the implementation of strategic methods, development of necessary skills, and ongoing improvement efforts, we can enable ourselves to make decisions that are consistent with our values, objectives, and aspirations. Making wise decisions turns into our compass as we negotiate the intricacies of life, pointing us in the direction of achievement and contentment.

The Behavioral Finance Advantage: Harnessing Psychology for Smarter Financial Decisions

Rationality has long been seen as the cornerstone of good decision-making in the financial industry. This conventional wisdom, however, has been called into question by recent developments in behavioral finance, which have shown how much psychological influences shape our financial decisions. People can have a big advantage in negotiating the difficulties of saving, investing, and managing their money by knowing how human behavior and financial decisions interact.

Unveiling the Behavioral Finance Advantage

The persistent departures from rational conduct that frequently characterize financial decisions are the subject of behavioral finance, an interdisciplinary field that combines economics and psychology. These variations, often referred to as behavioral biases, are caused by societal pressures, emotional triggers, and cognitive constraints that result in less-than-ideal decisions that may have far-reaching effects.

People can create plans to lessen the effects of these biases and make better financial decisions by being aware of them. With the help of this behavioral finance advantage, people can overcome their innate heuristics, or mental shortcuts, which frequently cause them to make rash or illogical decisions.

Common Behavioral Biases and Their Impact

Financial decision-making has been linked to a number of behavioral biases. Among the most well-known are:

- **Anchoring Bias**: the propensity to base subsequent decisions unduly on the initial piece of information one comes across, or the anchor.

- **Availability Bias:** the propensity to exaggerate the chance of things that are easier for us to imagine, frequently as a result of recent news reports or firsthand encounters.

- **Confirmation Bias:** The propensity to ignore contradicting facts and favor information that confirms our preexisting opinions is known as confirmation bias.

- **Hindsight Bias:** The propensity to overestimate our capacity for historical prediction, which frequently results in a delusion of certainty regarding our capacity for making decisions.

- **Loss Aversion:** The propensity to experience gains' joy more quickly than losses' sorrow, which results in risk-averse actions and lost chances.

These and other prejudices have a big influence on our financial decisions. Anchoring bias, for example, may result in asset overpayment or undervaluation of prospective investments. Whereas confirmation bias serves to maintain unfavorable investment methods and strengthen preexisting biases, availability bias can lead to overreaction to brief market movements.

Harnessing Behavioral Finance for Smarter Decisions

People can actively reduce the impact of these biases on their financial decisions by being aware of their existence. The following are some useful tactics to think about:

- **Seek out diverse perspectives:** Seek advice from financial professionals, seasoned investors, or reliable peers to disprove your own ideas and obtain alternative perspectives.

- **Establish clear financial goals:** Establish your long-term financial goals and a strategy to reach them. This can offer a foundation for logically assessing investing choices.

- **Employ decision-making tools:** Make decisions based on quantitative facts by using financial calculators, risk assessment instruments, and portfolio optimization software.

- **Incorporate emotional buffers:** Give yourself enough time to consider financial matters logically and calmly. Before making a decision, let your feelings settle.

- **Seek professional guidance**: Give yourself enough time to consider financial matters logically and calmly. Before making a decision, let your feelings settle.

The benefit of behavioral finance is that it enables people to identify and address the psychological influences on their financial decisions. People who are aware of the effects of biases and heuristics can devise plans for making better educated, logical, and ultimately profitable financial decisions. Gaining control over one's financial destiny, increased investment returns, and improved financial well-being are all possible outcomes of adopting behavioral finance concepts.

Building a Solid Foundation: Decision-Making Frameworks

Making wise decisions is essential in the dynamic world of finance since it helps one navigate the challenges of saving, investing, and handling personal money. Although economic principles and rationality are frequently emphasized in traditional financial theories, behavioral finance has recently made significant strides in highlighting the significant impact of psychological aspects on our financial decisions.

People can create a strong basis for making well-informed and logical financial decisions by integrating behavioral insights into well-established decision-making frameworks. These frameworks offer an organized method for weighing possibilities, taking risks, and matching financial decisions to long-term objectives.

Established Decision-Making Frameworks

Numerous well-established frameworks for decision-making have been widely acknowledged for their efficaciousness in diverse financial scenarios. These consist of:

- **Cost-Benefit Analysis:** With the use of this framework, prospective costs and benefits of each financial alternative are carefully considered, empowering people to make decisions based on a thorough evaluation of trade-offs.
- **Net Present Value (NPV) Analysis:** This approach is intended especially for the assessment of investment prospects. It provides a foundation for assessing various investment possibilities by taking the time value of money into account and figuring out the present value of future cash flows.
- **Risk-Return Analysis:** The paradigm recognizes that financial decisions inherently include a trade-off between risk and return. It aids in the assessment of possible risks related to various investment options and the determination

of whether possible returns outweigh potential dangers.

- **SMART Goals:** This framework provides a thorough way to define and achieve financial goals. It emphasizes the necessity of SMART goals—Specific, Measurable, Achievable, Relevant, and Time-bound—to ensure that targets are attainable, understandable, and consistent with individual circumstances.

- **Financial Planning:** A comprehensive approach to managing personal money is encompassed by this comprehensive framework. Together with making sure that investment decisions are in line with overall financial objectives, it entails budgeting, setting financial goals, building a savings plan, and making educated financial judgments.

Incorporating Behavioral Insights

Although these well-established frameworks offer a strong basis for logical financial decision-making, adding behavioral insights might increase their efficacy even further. Many biases and heuristics that might affect our financial decisions and frequently result in less-than-ideal outcomes have been found in the field of behavioral finance. People who are aware of these biases might devise ways to lessen their influence and make better decisions.

One way to counteract anchoring bias, for example, is to avoid using the first piece of information you come across as your only source of information when making decisions. Instead, acquire information from several sources. By actively looking for information that challenges our preconceived notions and taking a wider view of the situation, we can combat availability bias.

The Importance of a Systematic Approach

Adopting a systematic approach to financial decision-making offers several significant advantages:

- **Enhanced Decision Quality**:
- Making decisions based on a methodical approach decreases the probability of rash or unreasonable choices, resulting in better-informed and thoughtful selections.
- **Reduced Emotional Influence:**
  People can reduce the impact of emotions on their decision-making process by adhering to a systematic framework, which will guarantee that financial decisions are made with long-term objectives rather than short-term satisfaction.
- **Greater Confidence:**
  A methodical approach encourages people to feel confident while making financial decisions, enabling them to make well-informed decisions instead of depending mostly on instinct or gut feeling.

- **Improved Financial Outcomes:**
  A methodical approach to financial decision-making has the potential to produce superior financial results over time, such as more secure financial futures, more profitable investments, and more efficient budgeting. A methodical approach to financial decision-making has the potential to produce superior financial results over time, such as more secure financial futures, more profitable investments, and more efficient budgeting.

Breaking the Chains: Overcoming Psychological Barriers

Recognizing Typical Psychological Obstacles

Psychological obstacles frequently impede financial decision-making, impairing judgment and resulting in less-than-ideal decisions. These obstacles may appear in a number of ways, such as:

- **Fear:** Delay, hesitation, or missed chances might result from the fear of making a mistake or suffering financial loss.

- **Indecision:** An inability to make timely decisions due to overanalyzing information or feeling overwhelmed by choices can hinder progress and lead to regret.

- **Impulsivity:** Making snap judgments that might not be in line with financial objectives can come from acting on emotions or gut instincts without giving long-term effects enough thought.

Overcoming Impulsivity, Indecision, and Fear

Take into consideration some practical strategies to overcome these psychological obstacles and make wise financial decisions:

- **Face Your Fears:** Acknowledge your anxieties and deal with them head-on. Compile data, consult specialists, and create backup plans to reduce possible hazards.

- **Embrace Uncertainty:** Understand that financial decisions are inherently uncertain. Recognize that not every result can be predicted and concentrate on making decisions that are well-informed given the information at hand.

- **Establish Clear Goals:** Prioritize your financial objectives and explicitly define them. This will offer a structure for assessing options and selecting actions that are in line with your long-term goals.

- **Seek Expert Advice:** Seek advice from seasoned investors or financial consultants to obtain a variety of viewpoints and valuable insights.

- **Seek Emotional Support:** When faced with difficult financial decisions, confide in therapists, family members, or trustworthy friends for emotional support and to process your feelings.

The Adaptive Investor: Making Decisions in a Dynamic Environment

Adaptability in Financial Decision-Making

The financial environment is dynamic and ever-changing, necessitating flexibility in decision-making for optimal outcomes. The capacity to modify plans and choices in reaction to fresh information, shifting market conditions, and altering individual situations is known as adaptability.

Strategies for Adaptive Decision-Making

To become an adaptive investor, consider these strategies:

- **Continuously Update Your Knowledge:**

  Keep yourself updated on market movements, economic developments, and new investing opportunities.

- **Regularly Review Your Portfolio:** Periodically review your investment portfolio to make sure it still fits your financial objectives and current risk tolerance.

- **Be Prepared to Adjust Strategies:**

Be prepared to modify your investment strategies in reaction to notable changes in the market or in your own situation.

- **Embrace Technology:**

  To improve your decision-making process, make use of market analysis platforms, investment research tools, and financial planning software.

Your Decision Arsenal: Crafting a Personalized Toolkit

Building a Personalized Decision-Making Toolkit

To make wise financial decisions, you need a customized toolkit based on your learning preferences, risk tolerance, and financial objectives. You should have a variety of tools, materials, and techniques in your toolkit to enable you to confidently make well-informed decisions.

Examples of Tools and Resources

Your decision arsenal may include:

- **Financial Planning Software:** To analyze various investment possibilities, manage costs, and generate budgets, use financial planning software.

- **Investment Research Tools:** Use investment research tools to evaluate market trends, compare investment possibilities, and examine the financial statements of companies.

- **Risk Tolerance Assessment Tools:** Utilize risk tolerance assessment tools to determine your comfort level with different levels of investment risk.

- **Financial Education Resources:** Use resources for financial education to increase your knowledge and comprehension of financial ideas, including books, articles, and online courses..

Learning from the Pros: Real-World Case Studies

Case Studies in Strategic Decision-Making:

Case studies from the real world provide insightful information about how to make effective strategic decisions. We can learn a great deal about decision-making for ourselves by studying the ideas and deeds of seasoned investors and financial experts.

Analyzing Thought Processes and Extracting Valuable Lessons

When analyzing case studies, consider the following questions:

- • What aspects did the decision-maker take into account?

- How did the decision-maker assess risks and potential outcomes?

- • What tactics did the decision-maker use to get past obstacles?

- • What insights can be gained from the process of making decisions?

Emotional Intelligence in Decision-Making

Harnessing Emotional Intelligence

Making wise financial decisions is largely dependent on emotional intelligence (EI). Emotional intelligence (EI) is the capacity to identify, comprehend, and control emotions in both oneself and others. Strong emotional intelligence (EI) enables people to make more thoughtful and logical decisions even when faced with difficult circumstances or emotional triggers.

Enhancing Emotional Intelligence

Try the following to improve your emotional intelligence and help you make more emotionally smart financial decisions:

- **Develop Self-Awareness:** Acknowledge the impact of your own emotions on your decision-making.

- **Practice Empathy:** Recognize other people's viewpoints and feelings, particularly while making decisions that affect other people.

- **Manage Stress:** Determine useful stress-reduction strategies to keep feelings from impairing judgment.

decision-making processes, individuals can overcome inherent biases, make more informed choices, and ultimately achieve their financial goals with greater confidence and success.

CHAPTER SIX

The Family Financial Dynamic

"Family, Money, and Influence"

Families' relationships have a big impact on how people feel and behave when it comes to finances. This chapter explores the complex interactions that exist between financial decision-making and family dynamics. Specifically, it looks at the impact that communication styles, values, and upbringing have on our relationship with money.

Impact of Family Upbringing on Financial Habits

Inherited Money Mindsets:

- Examine the generational transmission of family money mindsets.
- Talk about how parents and grandparents influence people's financial attitudes.

- Case studies demonstrating how inherited financial views affect people.

Cultural and Socioeconomic Influences:
Examine how cultural and socioeconomic factors within a family influence financial decision-making.

- Talk about the ways that varying cultural upbringings can affect how people see money, spending, and saving.

- Techniques for handling possible disputes that may arise from different financial viewpoints in the family.

Strategies for Healthy Financial Conversations within Families

Open Communication:

- Emphasize the value of honest and open communication within the family regarding finances.

- Give advice on how to start financial conversations without getting into a fight..

- Give advice on how to start financial conversations without getting into a fight. Case studies illustrating the benefits of open communication.

Financial Goal Setting as a Family:

- Talk about the advantages of establishing and achieving financial goals together as a family.
- Give real-world examples of family financial objectives and how they can be cooperatively attained.
- Advice on coordinating personal goals with family finances as a whole.

Navigating Differences in Money Attitudes Among Family Members

Understanding Diverse Money Personalities:

- Present the idea of distinct financial personalities existing within a family.
- Examine methods for accommodating and respecting different financial choices.

- Case studies that show how to resolve disagreements about money can be successfully navigated.

Teaching Financial Literacy within the Family:

- Talk about how financial education can close the gap between different financial literacy levels in a family.
- Give family members access to tools and activities that will help them become more financially literate.
- Techniques for fostering a common knowledge of financial ideas and procedures.

Our financial life are greatly influenced by our families. Families can foster a healthy and encouraging atmosphere for financial success by comprehending the dynamics at work and putting excellent communication and teamwork techniques into practice. This chapter offers advice on how to help families get along financially and make sure that the family becomes a stronghold in the quest for financial security.

Discussion Points and Exercises:
Discussion starters that promote introspection on the financial dynamics of families.
Exercises that are useful for starting financial discussions in the family.

Recommendations for family financial activities to strengthen bonds and shared financial goals.

CHAPTER SEVEN

Investing in Yourself: Financial Education and Growth

The foundations of financial success in an ever-evolving financial environment are ongoing education and personal development. This chapter examines the vital role that financial education plays, offering tactics for continuous personal improvement as well as insights into the power of information.

The Imperative of Lifelong Learning

The Dynamic Financial Environment

It is essential to comprehend how dynamic financial markets and economic movements are. Examine how being educated enables people to respond proactively to changing situations by making decisions.

The Impact of Technology on Finance

Talk about how technology has revolutionized the banking sector. Examine how embracing technology changes can help you take advantage of new opportunities and overcome obstacles.

Resources for Continuous Financial Education

Books, Blogs, and Periodicals

Analyze the benefits of using digital and conventional resources to stay current on investing techniques, market movements, and financial news. Emphasize books, blogs, and reliable magazines that are suggested.

Online Courses and Webinars:

Consider the benefits of online courses and webinars for organized financial education. Discuss platforms, certifications, and the flexibility they offer to individuals with varying learning styles.

Networking and Professional Associations:

Stress the value of networking in the financial industry. Highlight the benefits of attending conferences, joining professional associations, and taking part in industry activities.

Integrating Financial Education into Personal Growth

Cultivating a Growth Mindset:

Analyze the connection between achieving financial success and having a growth mentality. Give helpful advice on cultivating a mindset that welcomes obstacles and sees mistakes as teaching moments.

Setting Personal Finance Goals:

Assist readers in establishing worthwhile and attainable financial objectives. Talk about how important it is to match these objectives with one's long-term goals and personal values.

Balancing Professional and Financial Growth:

Consider how people could successfully reconcile their pursuit of career achievement with their goal of financial security. Give guidance on picking a profession that would enable you to reach your financial objectives.

Overcoming Challenges in Financial Education

Information Overload:

In the digital era, address the problem of information overload. Provide methods for information filtering and prioritization so that a personalized learning experience can be created.

Time Constraints:

Acknowledge the time limits that people with hectic schedules must contend with. Incorporate useful time-management strategies into everyday activities to incorporate ongoing education.

CHAPTER EIGHT,

"Tomorrow's Money: "Future-Proofing Your Finances."

A journey through your financial future with a vision. In "Tomorrow's Money: Future-Proofing Your Finances," we set out to unravel the constantly changing financial scene and provide you with the knowledge and tactics required to prosper in the face of change.

Navigating Uncertainty: The Essence of Tomorrow's Money

Technological developments, economic upheavals, and sociological shifts are all driving significant change in the financial sector. This chapter provides a blueprint for adjusting your financial plans to the opportunities and difficulties that lie ahead, acting as your compass in these unknown waters.

Why Future-Proof Your Finances?

Financial future-proofing is not only a wise decision, but a strategic necessity in a world where change is inevitable. Your prosperity tomorrow is built on the financial choices you make now. Developing a resilient and flexible financial plan requires an awareness of and acceptance of the trends that will influence the future.

The Acceleration of Technological Trends

We first address the rapidly accelerating changes in technology as we get deeper into the chapter. Blockchain, fintech, and AI are more than simply catchphrases; they signify profound changes in how we handle money. We will discuss the implications for your wealth and how new technologies are changing the financial scene.

Economic Shifts: Beyond Borders and Boundaries

Economic environments change; they are never stagnant. The chapter lays out the landscape of changes in the world economy, looking at the emergence of emerging economies, the complexities of shifting trade patterns, and the influence of geopolitical events. Comprehending these changes is essential to creating a long-lasting financial strategy.

Adapting to Market Volatility: The Art of Resilience

While market volatility is inevitable, how you ride its waves matters greatly. You will leave this chapter with tactics to handle market volatility. We'll look at the psychology of market swings and provide strategies for thriving in the face of uncertainty as well as for weathering storms.

Tomorrow's Money, Sustainable Money

Future financial environments will prioritize purpose over mere profit. When we talk about how it's not only morally right but also financially sensible to match your investments with your principles, sustainable and impact investing take center stage. Find out how sustainable habits can help you maintain your financial stability over time.

Long-Term Planning for Financial Security: A Holistic Approach

The core of the issue is reached at the end of this chapter: long-term financial security planning. We will discuss wealth preservation, flexible approaches to responding to changes in the economy, health-related issues, and the significance of regular financial checkpoints in addition to retirement preparation.

Embark on the Journey

This chapter is an invitation to set out on a path of financial freedom and enlightenment, not merely a reading experience. Every page reveals fresh perspectives, doable tactics, and a comprehensive approach to future-proofing your finances. As we explore the nuances of tomorrow's financial landscape, never forget that you hold the ability to influence your own financial future.

CHAPTER NINE

Implementing Your Financial Blueprint

Implementation is a crucial phase in your financial journey. By now, you have created a customized financial plan and obtained deep understanding of the psychology of money. It's time to put theory into practice and achieve your financial objectives.

YOUR PERSONAL FINANCIAL PLAN

Crafting Your Financial Roadmap:

Your financial blueprint serves as your road map to financial success and is much more than a simple paper. We'll walk you through the process of turning your thoughts into a workable plan in this part. Let's examine:

- Determining precise and doable financial objectives.
- Determining both immediate and long-term goals.

- Keeping risk and reward in check when making investing decisions.

Measuring Progress

Monitoring and evaluating your progress is necessary for effective implementation. We'll examine:

- - Setting up key performance indicators (KPIs) in relation to your financial objectives.
- Consistent evaluations and modifications to guarantee you stay on path.
- - Honoring significant junctures along the path.

Executing Your Strategy

Building Financial Discipline:

- - Financial strategies that are successful must be disciplined. Learn techniques for:
- Overcoming typical behavioral obstacles to budgetary restraint.

- Fostering sound money management practices.
- Establishing a conducive atmosphere for methodical decision-making.

Executing Your Strategy

Building Financial Discipline:

Financial plans that are successful must be disciplined. Learn techniques for:

- Overcoming typical behavioral obstacles to sound money management.
- •Fostering sound money management practices.
- Establishing a conducive atmosphere for methodical decision-making.

Investment Tactics

Investments have a major role in implementation. Learn about:

• Choosing investment vehicles that fit your goals;

- Using diversification methods based on your risk tolerance;

- Managing your portfolio over time.

Recognizing Triggers

Building discipline requires knowing what sets off impulsive financial actions and recognizing those triggers. We'll go over how to identify emotional cues and other influences that could affect your financial decisions. Knowing these triggers will help you better navigate them and make decisions that support your long-term objectives.

Cultivating Positive Financial Habits

Developing disciplined behaviors that support your financial objectives is part of the process. We'll go into practical strategies for developing routines including consistent saves, routine budget reviews, and thoughtful spending. You'll lay a strong basis for long-term financial discipline by incorporating these routines into your life.

Creating a Supportive Environment

Your financial conduct is greatly influenced by the things around you. We'll help you establish a conducive environment that promotes financial restraint. This covers methods for creating a supportive work environment, interacting with motivated people, and reducing distractions that can divert your attention from your financial goals.

Adapting Your Investment Portfolio

The dynamism of financial markets should be reflected in your investment strategy. Learn how to modify your investing portfolio over time. We'll go over how to take advantage of fresh opportunities, and rebalance, and modify asset allocations in response to market conditions—all while adhering to your long-term financial goals.

Risk Management Strategies

Risk management and comprehension are essential for the efficient implementation of any financial plan. We'll explore risk management techniques to assist you in achieving the ideal ratio of reward to risk. Through the use of hedging strategies and stop-loss orders, you will acquire a thorough understanding of how to manage the inherent uncertainty of financial markets.

Staying Accountable

Accountability Partnerships

Being accountable is essential to success. Find out about:

- Creating an accountability partner network.
- Consulting financial advisors for expert advice.

- Making use of technology to enforce and monitor accountability.

Navigating Setbacks

No financial journey is without challenges. Gain insights into:

- Common failures and strategies for overcoming them.
- Modifying your plan to account for unforeseen circumstances.
- Preserving fortitude in the face of economic hardship.

Sustaining Long-term Success

Adapting to Life Changes

- Your financial plan should be dynamic, just like life itself. Examine: - Methods for modifying your plan in response to significant life occurrences.

- Maintaining a consistent yet flexible financial plan.
- Preparing and anticipating changes in the future.

Legacy planning is about your long-term influence on the world, not just your financial situation. This section will discuss the importance of legacy planning and offer helpful advice on how to leave a lasting and significant financial legacy.

Transferring Wealth and Estate Planning

A careful approach to estate preparation is the first step in legacy planning. We'll walk you through all the nuances involved in drafting an extensive estate plan, such as:

Trusts and Wills: Recognizing the value of a will and the different ways that trusts can be used to preserve and transfer assets.

Tax Efficiency: Techniques for reducing the tax consequences of wealth transfers so that your intended beneficiaries gain the most.

Charitable Giving: examining philanthropic opportunities in your estate plan and coordinating your legacy with worthy groups that share your beliefs.

Passing on Financial Knowledge

Your knowledge and wisdom are part of your legacy, which goes beyond financial wealth. We'll talk about how to:

Teach the Next Generation: Ways to help your descendants become financially literate so they can make wise decisions.

Family meetings: Encouraging candid and transparent conversations about expectations, beliefs, and money to help family members come to a mutual agreement.

Mentoring and Guidance: Giving family members or other community members continuing mentoring and sharing the things you've learnt from your financial path.

Leaving a Lasting Impact

Beyond material possessions, a significant legacy improves society and the globe. We'll look at:
- Socially Responsible Investing: Combining environmental and social concerns
- Thinks about how your investing plan can help bring about positive change.
- Founding Foundations and Endowments: To ensure a long-lasting influence for future generations, create philanthropic foundations or endowments to promote subjects you are passionate about.
- Documenting Your Legacy: How to use written texts, films, or other media to preserve

your family's heritage, morals, and distinctive experiences for future generations.

Planning for Transitions

Your legacy strategy should be adaptable enough to change as circumstances do. We'll talk about:

Succession Planning for Family Businesses:
ensuring that family companies pass smoothly to the following generation while striking a balance between innovation and continuity.

Adapting to Changing Circumstances:
Techniques for reviewing and modifying your legacy plan in light of shifting objectives, the state of the economy, or family relationships.

Legacy planning is a continuous process that calls for careful thought and flexibility.

It is not a one-time event. A legacy that lasts for generations can be left by carefully arranging for the transfer of both material and immaterial assets, which will benefit your family, your community, and the entire globe.

CHAPTER TEN

Conclusion

Thank you for finishing "Decoding the Psychology of Money: Mastering the Mind-Money Connection." Your dedication to financial empowerment has strengthened our community as a whole in addition to changing your perspective.

I now ask you to pause for a moment and return the favor.

Your Perspective Counts: Your reviews of the book serve as a guide for those who are thinking about taking this life-changing journey. Was there a passage that particularly spoke to you? Have you used a tactic that produced favorable outcomes? Your stories can help and motivate other readers to achieve financial mastery.

Advancing the Discussion: Not only are you sharing your experience when you leave a review, but you're also starting a dialogue. Your comments are incorporated into a lively conversation in our community, where a variety of viewpoints enhance each person's educational experience. Regardless of your level of experience with investing or familiarity with financial literature, your own perspective makes a significant addition.

Creating an Empowering Community: Reviews influence the community we're creating together more than just stars and comments. Your encouraging review contributes to the development of a community where people from different backgrounds can meet, exchange knowledge, and offer mutual support while navigating financial challenges.

How to Communicate Your Ideas:

1. Go to the website where you downloaded or bought the book.
2. Find the section for reviews.
3. Talk openly about your ideas and personal experiences.

Your evaluation serves as more than simply a feedback form; it's evidence of how hard we all work to become financially literate.

We appreciate your vital role in our community. Your opinion counts, and others may be motivated to start their own financial mastery path by reading your insightful commentary.

Warm regards,

[DR. JAKE JAYLEN]